PEAK PERFORMANCE

Mindful Self-Discipline for Optimal Achievement

BY

Dr. Lewis Grossberg

Contents

Introduction

Mindfulness, once considered a practice confined to meditation and relaxation, has now emerged as a potent tool for achieving and sustaining peak performance in various spheres of life. Its real-life applications span from boardrooms to classrooms, healthcare settings, and beyond, showcasing tangible benefits that transcend mere tranquility. Let's embark on a journey through the tangible impacts of mindfulness practices, exploring how this seemingly serene concept fuels remarkable achievements and fosters sustained excellence in diverse realms of human endeavor.

Chapter 1

Defining Peak Performance

Peak performance represents the pinnacle of one's abilities, where individuals consistently operate at their best across multiple facets of life. It's characterized by a state of optimal functioning, where individuals tap into their full potential to achieve outstanding results. This state isn't limited to a single area; it encompasses professional, personal, physical, and mental aspects, ensuring a holistic approach to excellence.

Peak performance isn't just about reaching a temporary high; it's about maintaining a consistent level of excellence over time. It involves a blend of skills, habits, mindset, and environment that enable individuals to consistently produce exceptional outcomes.

Significance of Mindful Self-Discipline
In the pursuit of peak performance, the integration of mindful self-discipline emerges as a pivotal factor. Mindfulness introduces the practice of being present, fully engaged, and aware of one's thoughts, emotions, and environment. It cultivates focus, clarity, and resilience, essential qualities for optimal performance. Self-discipline acts as the driving force that channels this mindfulness into action. It involves the ability to control impulses, persevere through challenges, and maintain consistency toward specific goals. When combined with mindfulness, self-discipline becomes a conscious and intentional effort, aligning actions and decisions with long-term objectives.

The synergy between mindfulness and self-discipline creates a powerful foundation for achieving and sustaining peak performance. It's not merely about pushing harder but rather about working smarter, with

6

intentionality and awareness, fostering a
state of flow and sustained excellence.

Importance Of Peak Performance:

1. Optimal Productivity:
Peak performance allows individuals to
operate at their highest capacity, enabling
them to accomplish tasks more efficiently
and effectively. By maximizing productivity,
individuals can achieve more in less time
while maintaining high-quality results.

2. Enhanced Goal Achievement:
When operating at peak performance,
individuals are better equipped to set,
pursue, and achieve their goals. They
exhibit heightened focus, determination, and
consistency, making them more likely to
attain both short-term objectives and long-
term aspirations.

3. Improved Mental Agility:

Peak performance is associated with mental sharpness, clarity, and agility. It allows individuals to think critically, make better decisions, and adapt swiftly to changing situations or challenges.

4. Elevated Professional Success:
In professional settings, attaining peak performance can lead to career advancement, increased recognition, and higher levels of success. It allows individuals to stand out among their peers by consistently delivering exceptional results.

5. Personal Growth and Fulfillment:
Achieving peak performance fosters personal growth and a sense of fulfillment. It enables individuals to push beyond their limits, constantly learn, and improve, leading to a more satisfying and purposeful life.

Benefits of Peak Performance:

1. Increased Confidence:
Peak performance breeds confidence. As individuals consistently achieve success, they gain confidence in their abilities, which positively impacts their self-esteem and willingness to take on new challenges.

2. Better Health and Well-being:
Peak performance often entails a focus on physical and mental well-being. Maintaining high-performance levels involves adopting healthy habits such as regular exercise, balanced nutrition, adequate sleep, and stress management, contributing to overall health.

3. Enhanced Relationships:
Performing at one's peak can positively impact relationships, both personally and professionally. It promotes effective communication, teamwork, and leadership skills, fostering better collaboration and understanding among individuals.

4. Resilience to Stress:
Individuals adept at peak performance often develop resilience to stress. Mindful practices incorporated into peak performance strategies help manage stress more effectively, leading to a more balanced and harmonious life.

5. Continuous Improvement and Innovation:
Peak performers have a mindset focused on growth and innovation. They consistently seek ways to improve themselves, their work, and their surroundings, fostering innovation and progress in various domains.

6. Higher Levels of Satisfaction:
Attaining peak performance creates a sense of accomplishment and satisfaction. The pursuit of excellence and the fulfillment derived from overcoming challenges contribute to a more rewarding and fulfilling life experience.

In essence, achieving peak performance goes beyond mere success in specific endeavors; it cultivates a holistic approach to life, enhancing various aspects of personal and professional well-being, ultimately leading to a more fulfilling and impactful existence.

This introduction sets the stage for understanding that peak performance isn't an elusive state reserved for a select few. Instead, it's an attainable state that individuals can access by integrating mindful self-discipline into their daily lives, ultimately unlocking their true potential across various domains.

Chapter 2

Understanding Mindful Self-Discipline

Exploring Mindfulness and Its Role

Mindfulness, as a foundational element of this synergy, involves being fully present and aware of one's thoughts, feelings, bodily sensations, and surroundings without judgment. It's about acknowledging the present moment, fostering a deeper understanding of oneself, and cultivating a non-reactive, observant mindset.

The role of mindfulness in mindful self-discipline is pivotal. By being present and aware, individuals can better recognize impulses, distractions, and unproductive patterns of behavior. Mindfulness serves as the anchor that prevents drifting into autopilot, allowing for conscious decision-making aligned with long-term goals.

Defining Self-Discipline in Achievement

Self-discipline complements mindfulness by harnessing this awareness into intentional action. It encompasses the ability to regulate one's behavior, thoughts, and emotions in service of one's goals. It's the capacity to maintain focus, stay committed, and consistently work towards desired outcomes despite challenges or distractions. Mindful self-discipline is not about rigidity or suppressing impulses but rather about understanding them and making conscious choices aligned with one's values and objectives. It involves acknowledging the impulses or distractions without being controlled by them, fostering a sense of autonomy and control over one's actions. Understanding the interplay between mindfulness and self-discipline sets the groundwork for fostering a more intentional and purpose-driven approach to daily actions. It encourages individuals to engage in practices that enhance both mindfulness and self-discipline, recognizing their symbiotic relationship in achieving and maintaining peak performance.

Understanding peak performance involves recognizing and leveraging various factors that contribute to achieving and sustaining high levels of excellence across different domains. These factors encompass psychological, physiological, environmental, and behavioral aspects. These elements are:

1. Mindset and Mental Factors:
Growth Mindset: Embracing a growth-oriented mindset is pivotal. Believing in the ability to learn, adapt, and improve fosters resilience and a willingness to push beyond perceived limits.

- Positive Psychology:

Cultivating a positive outlook and focusing on strengths and possibilities rather than limitations fuels motivation and mental resilience.

- Intrinsic Motivation:
 Identifying internal drivers like passion, purpose, and personal values that fuel continuous improvement and sustained effort toward goals.

2. Physical Well-being:
Fitness and Nutrition: Maintaining physical fitness through regular exercise and a balanced diet enhances energy levels, cognitive function, and overall well-being, contributing to peak performance.

- Rest and Recovery:
Prioritizing adequate sleep, relaxation, and downtime aids in rejuvenation, optimal cognitive function, and stress management.

3. Emotional Intelligence:

Emotional Regulation: Managing emotions effectively is crucial. Emotionally intelligent individuals can recognize, understand, and regulate their emotions, contributing to better decision-making and interpersonal interactions.

- Resilience:

Building emotional resilience helps navigate setbacks, stress, and challenges, fostering adaptability and maintaining focus during difficult times.

4. Behavioral Strategies:
Goal Setting: Setting clear, specific, and challenging yet attainable goals with defined action plans promotes focus and direction.

- Self-Discipline:

Cultivating habits, routines, and self-control techniques that enable consistent and focused effort toward goals.

- Time Management:

Efficiently allocating time and prioritizing tasks to maximize productivity and minimize distractions.

5. Environmental Factors:
Supportive Environment: Creating surroundings conducive to productivity, incorporating elements such as an organized workspace, supportive relationships, and a positive culture.

- Innovation and Learning Culture: Encouraging continuous learning, innovation, and openness to change within the environment fosters growth and adaptation.
Understanding and optimizing these factors can lead to a comprehensive approach to achieving peak performance. By recognizing the interplay between psychological, physical, emotional, behavioral, and environmental elements, individuals can develop strategies tailored to their unique

circumstances, fostering sustained excellence in their pursuits.

Chapter 3

The Psychology Behind Optimal Achievement

Mental Framework for Success

Achieving peak performance involves more than just acquiring skills or adopting specific behaviors. It's deeply rooted in the psychological framework that individuals develop. This section explores the mental aspects that contribute to optimal achievement.

- Growth Mindset:

Discuss the significance of having a growth mindset, where challenges are viewed as opportunities for growth rather than setbacks. Embracing a belief that abilities and intelligence can be developed through dedication and hard work fosters resilience and continuous improvement.

- Positive Psychology:

Highlighting the importance of positive thinking and its impact on performance. Positive psychology emphasizes strengths, virtues, and optimal functioning, directing attention toward what's going well rather than dwelling on limitations.

- Intrinsic Motivation:

Exploring the power of internal drive in fueling sustained performance. Intrinsic motivation, stemming from personal passion, purpose, or interest, often leads to deeper engagement and higher levels of achievement compared to external motivators.

Understanding these psychological underpinnings is crucial in fostering a mindset conducive to sustained excellence.

It involves cultivating a positive, growth-oriented perspective that embraces challenges, values effort and remains intrinsically driven toward achieving personal and professional goals.

The Power of Mindful Habits

Habits play a fundamental role in shaping behavior and performance. This part delves into the influence of habits on achieving and maintaining peak performance.

- Routine and Consistency:
Discuss the importance of establishing routines and consistent habits that support one's goals. Routine brings stability and predictability, while consistent habits build momentum and facilitate progress.

- Mindful Habit Formation:
Exploring how mindfulness contributes to habit formation. Mindfulness practices help individuals become more aware of existing

habits, enabling them to intentionally cultivate new, beneficial habits aligned with their aspirations.

Understanding the psychological factors behind optimal achievement and the role of mindful habits equips individuals with the awareness and tools to shape their mental framework and daily routines in ways that support sustained high performance.

Chapter 4

Developing Mindful Self-Discipline

Cultivating a Mindful Mindset

Developing a mindful mindset involves practicing awareness, presence, and intentionality in daily life. This section explores various methods and exercises aimed at fostering mindfulness.

- Mindfulness Practices:
Detailing mindfulness meditation, breathing exercises, and sensory awareness techniques. These practices encourage individuals to observe thoughts, emotions, and sensations without judgment, fostering a greater sense of clarity and focus.

- Daily Integration:

Emphasizing the importance of integrating mindfulness into daily routines. Simple activities like mindful eating, walking, or even listening can serve as opportunities to enhance awareness and presence in everyday life.

By cultivating a mindful mindset, individuals become more attuned to their experiences and better equipped to respond thoughtfully rather than react impulsively, thereby strengthening their self-discipline.

Practices for Strengthening Self-Discipline

Self-discipline, being the driving force behind mindful action, involves intentional practices to reinforce this trait.

- Goal-Setting Techniques:

Discuss effective goal-setting methods that promote clarity and commitment. Setting specific, measurable, and realistic goals while aligning them with personal values enhances motivation and self-discipline.

- Overcoming Procrastination:
Exploring strategies to tackle procrastination and distractions. Techniques such as the Pomodoro Technique, task prioritization, and breaking tasks into smaller, manageable steps help in maintaining focus and overcoming procrastination tendencies. By combining the cultivation of mindfulness with intentional practices for enhancing self-discipline, individuals create a powerful synergy that aligns their actions with their aspirations, fostering a proactive and purposeful approach to achieving their goals.

Chapter 5

Mindful Approaches to Goal Setting

Setting Clear and Attainable Goals
Effective goal setting is pivotal in the pursuit of peak performance. This section focuses on strategies to set meaningful, achievable, and motivating goals.

- SMART Goal Framework:
Detailing the SMART criteria (Specific, Measurable, Achievable, Relevant, Time-bound) for goal setting. Discussing how this framework ensures goals are well-defined and actionable.

- Alignment with Personal Values:
Emphasizing the importance of aligning goals with personal values and aspirations. When goals resonate with one's core

values, individuals are more likely to remain motivated and committed to achieving them.

- Mindfulness in Goal Clarity:
Exploring how mindfulness aids in clarifying and refining goals. Mindfulness practices, such as visualization and reflection, help individuals gain a deeper understanding of their aspirations and the steps required to attain them.

☐ Mindfulness in Goal Execution
Execution plays a crucial role in achieving set goals. This part discusses how mindfulness supports the implementation and pursuit of defined objectives.

- Staying Present in Tasks:
Highlighting the significance of staying present and focused during task execution. Mindfulness practices, such as attention to breath or task-centered mindfulness, aid in maintaining concentration and productivity.

- Adapting Mindfully:
Addressing the role of flexibility and adaptability in goal pursuit. Mindfulness enables individuals to embrace change, adjust strategies when needed, and learn from setbacks without losing sight of their ultimate objectives.
By integrating mindfulness into the goal-setting process and execution, individuals enhance their ability to set meaningful goals aligned with their values and consistently work towards achieving them with focus, adaptability, and resilience.

Time management and prioritization are fundamental skills crucial for achieving and sustaining peak performance across various endeavors. Here's an exploration of their significance:
1. Time Management:

a. Resource Optimization:
Effective time management involves optimizing the available time to maximize

productivity. It's about allocating time to tasks based on their importance and urgency, ensuring the most crucial activities receive adequate attention.

b. Productivity Enhancement:
Prioritizing tasks and managing time efficiently boosts productivity. By focusing on high-value tasks and minimizing time spent on less critical activities, individuals can achieve more in less time.

c. Stress Reduction:
Proper time management reduces stress. When individuals have a clear plan and schedule, they're less likely to feel overwhelmed by deadlines or constantly rush to complete tasks, fostering a more relaxed and focused mindset.

d. Improved Decision-making:
Effective time management allows for thoughtful decision-making. When individuals have adequate time to assess

situations and options, they can make more informed choices, leading to better outcomes.

2. Prioritization:
a. Identifying High-Value Tasks:
Prioritization involves recognizing tasks or activities that contribute most significantly to one's goals. It helps distinguish between what's important and what's merely urgent, ensuring the focus remains on high-impact tasks.

b. Focus on Results:
Prioritization directs attention toward tasks that yield the most significant results. By focusing efforts on tasks that align with overarching goals, individuals can achieve meaningful progress.

c. Resource Allocation:
It enables the allocation of time, energy, and resources to activities that generate the most value. Prioritizing allows individuals to

invest their resources efficiently, maximizing output while minimizing unnecessary efforts.

d. Adaptability and Flexibility:
Effective prioritization allows for adaptability. It enables individuals to reprioritize tasks based on changing circumstances, ensuring that efforts align with current needs and goals.

Relationship to Peak Performance:

Time management and prioritization are integral components of achieving and sustaining peak performance:

- **Efficiency and Effectiveness:**
Effective time management ensures tasks are completed efficiently, while prioritization guarantees that the right tasks are tackled to achieve optimal results.

- **Consistency and Focus:**

Proper time management fosters consistency in effort, and prioritization maintains focus on tasks critical for success, promoting sustained high performance.

- Goal Alignment:

Both skills ensure efforts are aligned with overarching goals, preventing distractions and guiding individuals toward their desired outcomes.

In essence, mastering time management and prioritization is key to unlocking sustained peak performance. These skills enable individuals to channel their efforts toward the most impactful activities, optimize productivity, reduce stress, and maintain focus on what truly matters in their pursuit of excellence.

Resilience and stress management are crucial elements that significantly impact an individual's ability to achieve and sustain peak performance.

Resilience:

1. Adaptability and Flexibility:
Resilience involves the capacity to adapt
and bounce back from setbacks or
challenges. It's the ability to remain
composed and effectively navigate through
adversity, enabling individuals to stay
focused on their goals despite obstacles.

2. Emotional Strength and Coping Skills:
Resilient individuals possess robust
emotional strength and coping mechanisms.
They can manage stress, regulate
emotions, and maintain a positive outlook
even in demanding situations.

3. Optimism and Growth Mindset:
Resilience is closely linked to an optimistic
outlook and a growth mindset. Those with
resilience often view setbacks as
opportunities for growth rather than
insurmountable obstacles.

4. Risk-Taking and Learning from Failure:

Resilient individuals are more willing to take calculated risks and are not deterred by failures. Instead, they learn from setbacks, adapt their strategies, and apply these lessons to future endeavors.

Stress Management:

1. Awareness and Recognition:
Effective stress management begins with recognizing stress triggers and understanding their impact on performance. Being aware allows individuals to implement strategies to mitigate stressors.

2. Mindfulness and Relaxation Techniques:
Mindfulness practices, relaxation exercises, and deep breathing techniques are valuable tools in managing stress. These practices aid in calming the mind, reducing anxiety, and promoting a sense of well-being.

3. Time Management and Prioritization:

Organizing tasks, setting priorities, and managing time efficiently can significantly reduce stress levels. Having a clear plan and structure helps individuals approach tasks with less pressure.

4. Self-Care and Work-Life Balance: Balancing work commitments with personal life, hobbies, and relaxation activities is crucial for managing stress. Engaging in self-care routines nurtures mental and physical well-being, combating stress effectively.

Relationship to Peak Performance:

- Resilience and Adaptability:

Resilience enables individuals to weather challenges, maintain focus, and adapt to changing circumstances without compromising performance quality.

- Stress Management and Clarity of Mind:

Effectively managing stress ensures a clear and focused mindset. When stress is managed, individuals can concentrate better, make informed decisions, and sustain optimal performance levels.

- Consistency and Longevity:

Both resilience and stress management contribute to sustaining peak performance over the long term. They foster a sustainable approach to achieving high performance without burning out.

In conclusion, resilience and effective stress management play pivotal roles in sustaining peak performance. By developing resilience and implementing stress management techniques, individuals can navigate challenges effectively, maintain focus, and perform at their best consistently.

Chapter 6.

Mind-Body Connection in Performance

Balancing Mental and Physical Health
Optimal performance isn't solely reliant on mental prowess; it's deeply intertwined with physical well-being. This section emphasizes the symbiotic relationship between mental and physical health in achieving peak performance.

- Physical Fitness's Impact:
Discussing the role of physical fitness in mental acuity and overall performance. Regular exercise not only enhances physical health but also positively influences cognitive functions, mood regulation, and stress reduction.

- **Nutrition and Mental Clarity:**
Exploring the impact of nutrition on cognitive function and focus. Nutrient-dense diets rich in essential vitamins and minerals contribute to mental clarity, sustained energy levels, and improved overall well-being.
Importance of Rest and

- **Recovery:**
Highlighting the significance of adequate sleep and recovery in optimizing performance. Quality sleep and adequate downtime allow the body and mind to rejuvenate, enhancing cognitive function, decision-making, and emotional resilience.

Mindful Approaches to Fitness and Nutrition

This part delves deeper into incorporating mindfulness into fitness routines and dietary habits to support peak performance.

- **Mindful Eating Practices:**

Exploring mindful eating habits such as paying attention to hunger cues, savoring food, and eating with awareness. This approach fosters a healthier relationship with food and encourages better nutrition choices.

- Mindful Exercise:

Discussing the incorporation of mindfulness into physical workouts. Techniques like mindful movement, body awareness, and focused breathing during exercise sessions contribute to improved performance and reduced stress.

By acknowledging and nurturing the intimate connection between mental and physical health, individuals can adopt holistic approaches that synergistically enhance both aspects, fostering a solid foundation for sustained peak performance.

Optimizing physical health is a cornerstone for achieving and sustaining peak performance. This involves focusing on exercise and fitness, nutrition and diet, as well as sleep and recovery. Here's an exploration of each aspect:

Exercise and Fitness:

1. Physical Conditioning:
Regular exercise improves cardiovascular health, muscular strength, endurance, and flexibility. It enhances overall physical fitness, enabling individuals to perform at their peak.

2. Mental Clarity and Focus:
Exercise stimulates the release of endorphins, reducing stress and improving mood. This promotes mental clarity, focus, and concentration, which are crucial for sustained high performance.

3. Energy Levels and Stamina:
Engaging in regular physical activity increases energy levels and endurance. Enhanced stamina allows individuals to

maintain productivity and focus throughout the day.

Nutrition and Diet:

1. Fueling the Body:
A balanced diet comprising a variety of nutrients fuels the body for optimal performance. It provides the necessary energy, vitamins, minerals, and antioxidants essential for physical and mental functions.

2. Brain Health and Cognitive Function:
Nutrient-rich diets support brain health and cognitive function. Omega-3 fatty acids, antioxidants, and other nutrients aid memory, concentration, and overall mental sharpness.

3. Balancing Macronutrients:
A balanced intake of carbohydrates, proteins, and fats supports sustained energy levels and muscle recovery. Proper

macronutrient balance aids in both physical and mental performance.

Sleep and Recovery:

1. Restoration and Healing:
Quality sleep is crucial for the body's repair and recovery processes. It allows muscles to heal, consolidates learning, and enhances overall well-being.

2. Cognitive Functions and Decision-making:
Sufficient sleep is linked to better cognitive functions, including problem-solving, decision-making, and creativity. Adequate rest supports mental clarity and performance.

3. Stress Reduction and Emotional Balance:
Restorative sleep reduces stress hormones and promotes emotional balance. It contributes to a stable mood and reduces the likelihood of burnout.

- **Physical Resilience:**
Optimal physical health builds resilience, enabling individuals to endure challenging situations without fatigue or decreased performance.

- **Energy and Focus:**
Exercise, proper nutrition, and adequate sleep provide the energy needed for sustained focus and concentration required for peak performance.

- **Recovery and Sustainability:**
Adequate recovery through sleep and balanced nutrition sustain energy levels, preventing burnout and ensuring consistent high performance over time.
In summary, optimizing physical health through exercise, nutrition, and quality sleep is foundational for achieving and sustaining

peak performance. By prioritizing these aspects, individuals can enhance their physical and mental capacities, enabling them to consistently perform at their best.

Chapter 7

Mindfulness Practices for Optimal Performance

Meditation and Mindfulness Techniques
This section focuses on various meditation practices and mindfulness techniques tailored to enhance cognitive abilities, reduce stress, and improve overall performance.

- Mindfulness Meditation:
Exploring mindfulness meditation practices such as focused breathing, body scan meditation, or loving-kindness meditation.

These practices cultivate present-moment awareness, reduce stress, and promote mental clarity.

- Visualization Techniques: Discussing the power of visualization in achieving peak performance. Visualizing success, imagining optimal outcomes, and mentally rehearsing tasks contribute to enhanced focus and confidence. Breathwork for Stress Reduction: Highlighting the role of breathwork in managing stress and enhancing resilience. Breathing exercises, like diaphragmatic breathing or box breathing, help regulate emotions and maintain composure under pressure.

Enhancing Focus and Concentration
This part delves into strategies and techniques aimed at improving concentration and sustaining focus, crucial elements for achieving peak performance.

- **Attention Control Exercises:**
Discuss exercises that strengthen attention and focus, such as mindfulness-based attention training or selective attention exercises. These techniques aid in reducing distractions and improving concentration.

- **Minimizing Cognitive Load:**
Exploring methods to reduce cognitive overload and enhance cognitive resources. Techniques like task batching, prioritization, and creating optimal work environments help in managing mental resources effectively.

- **Mindful Breaks and Rest:**
Emphasizing the importance of incorporating mindful breaks and rest periods into daily routines. Mindful pauses or short breaks aid in rejuvenating the mind, enhancing productivity, and preventing mental fatigue.

By incorporating these mindfulness
practices into daily life, individuals can
cultivate a heightened sense of awareness,
sharpen their focus, and manage stress
more effectively, thereby enhancing their
overall performance in various aspects of
life.

Chapter 8

Emotional Intelligence and Mindful Achievement

Managing Emotions for Performance
This section delves into the significance of emotional intelligence in optimizing performance and explores techniques to manage emotions effectively.

- Understanding Emotions:
Discussing the importance of recognizing and understanding emotions. Emotional awareness allows individuals to navigate their feelings more effectively, enabling better decision-making and interpersonal interactions.

- Emotion Regulation Techniques:
Exploring strategies to regulate emotions during high-pressure situations. Techniques like deep breathing, reframing thoughts, or utilizing mindfulness practices help in maintaining emotional balance and focus.

- Stress Management:
Addressing stress management techniques for emotional well-being. Mindfulness-based stress reduction (MBSR) practices, relaxation exercises, and time management strategies aid in mitigating stressors that impact performance.

Developing Emotional Resilience

Building emotional resilience is crucial in sustaining optimal performance amidst challenges and setbacks. This part focuses on strengthening resilience through mindful practices.

- **Adaptability and Flexibility:**
Emphasizing the importance of adaptability and flexibility in facing adversity. Mindful approaches encourage individuals to embrace change, pivot when necessary, and maintain composure in dynamic environments.

- **Learning from Setbacks:**
Discuss how mindfulness supports learning from failures or setbacks. Encouraging a non-judgmental reflection on experiences fosters resilience, growth, and the ability to bounce back stronger.

- **Cultivating Optimism:**
Exploring mindfulness-based techniques to foster a positive outlook. Practicing gratitude, positive affirmations, and focusing on solutions instead of dwelling on problems contribute to a resilient mindset.
By integrating emotional intelligence with mindfulness practices, individuals can enhance their ability to understand,

manage, and leverage emotions effectively, thereby fortifying their emotional resilience and optimizing their overall performance.

Certainly! Handling pressure and anxiety while building confidence are essential aspects of achieving and maintaining peak performance. Here's an exploration of these factors:

Handling Pressure and Anxiety:

1. Mindfulness and Stress Reduction: Engaging in mindfulness practices, such as meditation and deep breathing, helps manage stress and reduce anxiety. These techniques promote a calm and centered mindset, allowing individuals to navigate pressure more effectively.

2. Effective Time Management: Structuring tasks and managing time efficiently can alleviate pressure. Breaking

down tasks into manageable parts and adhering to a schedule reduces the feeling of being overwhelmed.

3. Positive Self-Talk and Perspective:
Adopting a positive mindset and reframing challenges as opportunities for growth help alleviate anxiety. Positive self-talk and affirmations contribute to building resilience against pressure.

4. Seeking Support and Communication:
Talking to mentors, colleagues, or trusted individuals about pressures and anxieties can provide valuable perspectives and support. Effective communication aids in managing stress and finding solutions.

Building Confidence:

1. Setting Achievable Goals:
Setting and achieving realistic goals gradually builds confidence. Each

accomplishment reinforces belief in one's abilities and fosters a sense of achievement.

2. Competence and Skill Development:
Enhancing skills through continuous learning and practice boosts confidence. Developing expertise in a particular area provides a strong foundation for self-assurance.

3. Visualizing Success and Past Accomplishments:
Visualization techniques and reflecting on past successes instill confidence. Imagining successful outcomes and remembering past achievements reinforces a positive self-image.

4. Stepping Out of Comfort Zones:
Challenging oneself and taking calculated risks outside the comfort zone nurtures confidence. Embracing new experiences fosters personal growth and belief in one's abilities to overcome challenges.

Relationship to Peak Performance:

Pressure and Anxiety

- Management:

Handling pressure and anxiety effectively prevents these emotions from impeding performance, allowing individuals to stay focused and perform optimally.

- Confidence as a Performance Booster:

Confidence acts as a catalyst for peak performance. When individuals believe in their abilities, they're more likely to take on challenges, make bold decisions, and perform at their best.

- Resilience and Adaptability:

Confidence and the ability to handle pressure and anxiety contribute to resilience. Individuals with confidence navigate challenges more effectively, adapt quickly, and maintain high-performance levels despite adversity.

In essence, managing pressure and anxiety while building confidence are crucial components of achieving and sustaining peak performance. Cultivating strategies to handle stress, boosting self-assurance, and nurturing a positive mindset create an environment conducive to optimal performance across various aspects of life.

Chapter 9

Creating a Supportive Environment

Building a Mindful Workspace
This section focuses on optimizing the physical and psychological workspace to foster mindfulness and productivity.

- Ergonomics and Organization: Discussing the importance of ergonomic workspaces and organized environments. Comfortable and organized settings reduce distractions, promote focus, and support overall well-being.

  - Incorporating Mindfulness in the Workspace:

Exploring ways to integrate mindfulness into the work environment. Designing dedicated spaces for relaxation, incorporating natural elements, or implementing brief mindfulness practices within the workday contribute to a more mindful workspace.

- Encouraging Breaks and Movement: Highlighting the significance of taking regular breaks and incorporating movement into the work routine. Mindful breaks, stretching exercises, or short walks aid in rejuvenation and prevent burnout.

Cultivating Positive Relationships

This part delves into the importance of fostering positive interactions and relationships in achieving and maintaining peak performance.

- Communication and Collaboration:

Discussing effective communication strategies and fostering a collaborative atmosphere. Clear communication channels, active listening, and constructive feedback contribute to a supportive work environment.

- Team Dynamics:

Exploring the impact of positive team dynamics on performance. Encouraging a culture of trust, cooperation, and shared goals enhances team productivity and individual performance.

- Supportive Networks:

Emphasizing the value of supportive networks both within and outside the workplace. Building connections, mentorships, and a network of individuals who inspire and support personal growth contribute to sustained peak performance. By optimizing the physical workspace and nurturing positive relationships and collaborations, individuals can create an environment conducive to mindfulness, creativity, and mutual support, ultimately enhancing their overall performance and well-being.

Chapter 10

Strategies for Sustaining Mindful Peak Performance

Continuous Learning and Adaptation
This section emphasizes the importance of ongoing learning and adaptability as key components in sustaining peak performance.

- Lifelong Learning Mindset:
Discussing the value of adopting a mindset that embraces continuous learning and growth. Seeking new knowledge, acquiring new skills, and staying updated with industry trends fosters adaptability and innovation.

- Flexibility and Adaptation:

Exploring the necessity of adapting to changing circumstances. Mindful adaptation involves remaining open to change, being agile in decision-making, and adjusting strategies when necessary to maintain optimal performance.

Adaptability and flexibility

Adaptability and flexibility are pivotal strategies for individuals aiming to sustain peak performance over time. These qualities enable individuals to navigate evolving circumstances, challenges, and opportunities, ensuring consistently high performance. Here's an exploration of their significance:

Adaptability:

1. Embracing Change:

Adaptability involves embracing change rather than resisting it. Adaptable individuals readily adjust to new situations, technologies, or demands, ensuring they remain effective despite shifts in their environment.

2. Learning Agility:
Being adaptable requires a continuous learning mindset. Individuals who can quickly learn new skills, acquire knowledge, and adapt their strategies based on new information or experiences are better equipped to sustain peak performance.

3. Resilience to Setbacks:
Adaptable individuals bounce back from setbacks more readily. They view failures as opportunities for growth, learn from their experiences, and adjust their approaches to overcome challenges.

Flexibility:
1. Openness to Change:
Flexibility involves being open and receptive to change. Flexible individuals can easily pivot, modify their plans, and explore new

approaches without feeling overwhelmed or rigidly attached to one way of doing things.

2. Agile Decision-Making:
Flexibility allows for agile decision-making. Flexible individuals can quickly assess situations, consider various options, and make informed decisions even in rapidly changing or ambiguous environments.

3. Adaptation in Communication and Collaboration:
Flexibility extends to communication and collaboration. Those who are flexible in their interactions can easily adjust their communication style, adapt to diverse personalities, and foster productive collaborations across different contexts.

Relationship to Sustaining Peak Performance:

- Resilience in Adversity:

Adaptability and flexibility contribute to resilience. Individuals who can adapt to changes and flexibly adjust their strategies are more resilient, enabling them to sustain their performance despite unexpected challenges.

- Innovation and Creativity:
Being adaptable and flexible fosters innovation. Individuals who embrace new ideas and are open to different perspectives are more likely to innovate, introducing new methods or solutions that enhance their performance.

- Continuous Improvement:
Adaptability and flexibility facilitate continuous improvement. Those who are adaptable continuously seek ways to refine their approaches, embrace new tools, and stay ahead in their field, ensuring sustained high performance.
In essence, adaptability and flexibility are essential strategies for individuals striving to

sustain peak performance. By fostering
these qualities, individuals remain agile,
resilient, and open to change, positioning
themselves to consistently excel in dynamic
and evolving environments.

- Embracing Feedback:

Encouraging the utilization of feedback as a
tool for growth. Mindful consideration of
feedback, both constructive and critical, aids
in personal and professional development,
facilitating continuous improvement.

Avoiding Burnout through Mindful Practices

Addressing the importance of preventing
burnout and maintaining well-being while
striving for peak performance.

- Self-Care and Boundaries:

Highlighting the significance of setting
boundaries and practicing self-care. Mindful
self-care routines, such as taking breaks,

prioritizing rest, and nurturing hobbies or interests, safeguard against burnout.

- Work-Life Integration:
Discussing strategies for harmonizing work and personal life. Mindful integration involves creating a balanced routine that allows for fulfilling both professional and personal aspirations without compromising well-being.

- Stress Recognition and Management:
Emphasizing the need to recognize and manage stress proactively. Mindful stress management techniques, such as meditation, relaxation exercises, and time management, help in maintaining equilibrium amid challenges.

By adopting a mindset of continuous learning, adaptability, and prioritizing mindful practices that prevent burnout, individuals can sustain their peak performance over time, ensuring a balance

between high achievement and personal
well-being.

Chapter 11

Real-life Applications of Mindfulness in Achievement

Mindfulness has increasingly found real-life applications in various domains, demonstrating its profound impact on achieving and sustaining peak performance. Here's an exploration of how mindfulness practices translate into real-life results:

1. Enhanced Focus and Concentration:

☐ Real-life Application:
In workplaces, mindfulness techniques, such as focused breathing or attention training, improve employees' focus on tasks, minimizing distractions, and enhancing productivity.

☐ Results:
Individuals experience heightened concentration, allowing them to complete tasks efficiently and with greater accuracy, contributing to sustained peak performance.

2. Stress Reduction and Emotional Regulation:

☐ Real-life Application:
Mindfulness-based stress reduction programs in corporate settings or educational institutions help individuals manage stress and regulate emotions effectively.

☐ Results:
Reduced stress levels lead to a more composed mindset, improved decision-making, and better handling of pressure, fostering consistent high performance.

3. Improved Cognitive Function and Creativity:

☐ Real-life Application:
Mindfulness practices, including meditation and mindful exercises, are applied in creative industries and educational settings to stimulate creativity and innovative thinking.

☐ Results:
Enhanced cognitive abilities, such as improved problem-solving, heightened creativity, and increased mental clarity, contribute to innovative solutions and sustained peak performance.

4. Better Interpersonal Relationships:
☐ Real-life Application:
Mindfulness practices are utilized in team-building exercises, leadership training, and conflict-resolution workshops to improve communication and relationships.

☐ Results:

Improved interpersonal interactions foster a collaborative environment, enhancing teamwork, trust, and mutual understanding, leading to better overall performance.

5. Resilience and Adaptability:
Real-life Application: Mindfulness training is applied in high-stress environments, such as healthcare or emergency services, to build resilience and enhance adaptability.

☐ Results:

Individuals develop resilience to stress, maintain composure in challenging situations, and adapt swiftly, ensuring sustained high performance even in demanding circumstances.

6. Improved Well-being and Work-Life Balance:
☐ Real-life Application:

Incorporating mindfulness practices into daily routines fosters a sense of well-being and work-life balance.

☐ Results:
Individuals experience reduced burnout, improved mental health, and a balanced approach to life, enhancing overall performance in both professional and personal domains.

Relationship to Peak Performance:

• Consistency and Longevity:
Real-life applications of mindfulness demonstrate that individuals practicing mindfulness experience sustained and consistent high performance over time.

• Adaptability and Resilience:

Mindfulness practices cultivate adaptability and resilience, enabling individuals to

navigate challenges and maintain peak
performance despite dynamic environments.

- Holistic Well-being:
Mindfulness contributes to holistic well-being, encompassing mental, emotional, and physical aspects, providing a solid foundation for sustained optimal performance across various facets of life.
In summary, mindfulness practices have tangible real-life applications across different areas, yielding concrete results that foster sustained peak performance by enhancing focus, reducing stress, promoting resilience, and improving overall well-being.

CONCLUSION

In conclusion, the real-life applications of mindfulness for achieving and sustaining peak performance underscore its transformative impact across various domains. From corporate settings to educational institutions, healthcare, and personal development, mindfulness practices have showcased tangible benefits and results.

The incorporation of mindfulness techniques has proven instrumental in enhancing focus, reducing stress, fostering emotional regulation, and stimulating creativity. These outcomes directly contribute to improved cognitive functions, resilient decision-making, and heightened interpersonal relationships, ultimately fostering an environment conducive to sustained peak performance.

Moreover, mindfulness not only cultivates adaptability and resilience but also supports a holistic approach to well-being, promoting a balanced work-life integration and nurturing mental, emotional, and physical health.

The real-life applications of mindfulness affirm its role as a catalyst for excellence, enabling individuals to navigate challenges, maintain focus, and thrive in dynamic environments. As mindfulness continues to be integrated into diverse spheres of life, its profound impact on sustained peak performance becomes increasingly evident, shaping a future where mindfulness is a cornerstone of enduring success and well-being.